REAL ESTATE

PASSIVE INCOME

REAL ESTATE INVESTING, PROPERTY DEVELOPMENT, FLIPPING HOUSES

Second Edition
J.P. Richardson

© 2016

COPYRIGHT NOTICE

All rights reserved.

No part of this publication may be reproduced, distributed, or transmitted in any form or by any means; including, photocopying, recording, or other electronic or mechanical methods, without the prior written permission of the publisher, except in the case of brief quotations embodied in critical reviews and certain other non-commercial uses permitted by copyright law.

DISCLAIMER

Although the author and publisher have made every effort to ensure that the information in this book was correct at press time, the author and publisher do not assume and hereby disclaim any liability to any party for any loss, damage, or disruption caused by errors or omissions, whether such errors or omissions result from negligence, accident, or any other cause.

Table of Contents

COPYRIGHT NOTICE ii

DISCLAIMER iii

TABLE OF CONTENTS iv

INTRODUCTION 1

CHAPTER 1 – FINANCING YOUR REAL ESTATE
INVESTMENT 4

CHAPTER 2 – THE RIGHT INVESTMENT TYPE 28

CHAPTER 3 – CHOOSING THE RIGHT PROPERTY 34

CHAPTER 4 – BUILDING YOUR REAL ESTATE PASSIVE
INCOME 45

CHAPTER 5 – THE WORLD OF PROPERTY DEVELOPMENT 51

CHAPTER 6 – THE ART OF FLIPPING HOUSES 56

CHAPTER 7 – MANAGING & DIVERSIFYING YOUR
PORTFOLIO 60

CHAPTER 8 – COMMON MISTAKES TO AVOID WHEN
INVESTING IN REAL ESTATE 65

CONCLUSION 78

Introduction

Real estate investment is the process of purchasing a property with the intention of increasing your net worth. Purchasing a property to live in is one form of investment, although this is not a route that will usually lead to a passive income and a career in real estate. However, there are people who argue that purchasing a home is a form of investment and should be seen as the first step on the investment ladder. Your own property can, in future years, provide you with the capital you need to start purchasing other properties. It can even be kept when you purchase your next property and be rented; another way of making it your first step on the real estate investment ladder.

Generally, property investors look to build a collection of houses, apartments and even commercial buildings; each of these properties is expected to provide a return on the original investment. There are several ways in which you can make money from property; a passive income can be generated by purchasing properties and renting them out to individuals and businesses. The less work you are required to do to earn money the more passive the income. Alternatively funds can be earned via the more lucrative, but more risky, approach of flipping properties or even becoming involved in property development.

Real estate investment has come into the limelight in recent years, despite the difficult recession, property prices are now on the rise again. Investors who plan carefully can avoid the detrimental effects of the recession by hanging onto their assets and waiting for them to increase in value again. Providing you plan carefully and are able to cover the cost of any finance, a recession can actually increase the passive income available. As people fall onto hard times and have their own homes repossessed they will need somewhere to rent; the property portfolio you build can provide just the accommodation they need. Of course, if you have not planned your strategy properly you can lose your properties and be the one in need of a home.

It is essential to remember that, when generating a passive income, you are generally creating long term investment options. These can be very resistant to market changes. House flipping and property development are short term investment options and are much more vulnerable to the current state of the market. This is one of the reasons it is so important to diversify your portfolio and create a strong position for yourself against any market development.

This book will cover the different types of real estate investment and the different methods of financing them, this includes details of how to locate the relevant lenders and secure the necessary funds. It will also take a look at building a passive income from property, what is involved in the world of property development, how to successfully flip houses and the best way of managing and diversifying a property portfolio. Perhaps most importantly, it will provide you with a guide as what makes a property worth investing in and what warning signals you should pay attention to so as to avoid making a bad investment.

Real Estate Investing can be a lucrative and interesting career but it is not the right choice for everyone. At times it is hard work; you will have financial obligations which need to be met whether you have tenants or not; you will also encounter bad tenants who will end up needing to be evicted; an expensive and time consuming process. This book will help you to evaluate whether you wish to pursue real estate investment as either a career or a means to save for retirement.

As with most specialist subjects it is important to learn as much as possible concerning the industry before you start investing; the more you understand how the industry works and the potential pitfalls the better prepared you will be to make a success of your endeavors. The final section in this book provides some useful tips on real estate investment mistakes to be avoided; you will find it beneficial!

Chapter 1 – Financing Your Real Estate Investment

To invest in real estate you need to have funds available. There is no such thing as a free house! The first thought that springs to your mind will probably be to see your bank and enquire about a mortgage; whilst this is an option it is not necessarily the best option for your needs. There are a variety of methods which can be utilized to create the necessary funds for your business venture:

Using 'Cash'

Cash does not literally mean a briefcase full of cash! All funds are electronic and dealt with via a bank transfer, banker's draft, or in rare cases a personal cheque. In simple terms, someone who purchases with cash is someone who has immediate funds available. They have no need to borrow capital from another source. This method of purchasing real estate is relatively straightforward, subject to money laundering rules. It eliminates the need to pay interest or any fees on the capital needed and makes property investment a relatively safe bet. Having no finance means that should you wish to sell, you will always be able to wait until prices have improved. Alternatively you can take a loss on your investment and still have some cash in your hand.

However, it is important to consider whether a cash purchase is the right method for your needs as an investor.

- Firstly, if you are fortunate enough to have enough cash to purchase a property outright you must consider whether you are leaving yourself enough cash to cover any emergencies which may arise. This may be property related emergencies or personal ones.

- Secondly, property can be difficult to sell, whilst you own the property your funds cannot be accessed unless you either sell or remortgage the property. This could make it very difficult if you need some or all of your capital in a hurry.

- Thirdly, a property is a sizeable investment. Whilst you should obtain a good return on your investment this may not be the most efficient use of your capital. Your money will earn interest if you purchase treasury bonds and this could be a supplement to your property income. Alternatively, the funds you have available may be better used as a deposit on several houses, immediately boosting your game and increasing both your portfolio and your income potential.

- Fourthly, your exposure is lower. If something terrible goes wrong and the funds from your property are needed then being forced to sell at a low price could cost you a chunk of your capital and actually make you worse off. Purchasing the property with a loan means that less of your personal funds are exposed; should anything go wrong.

It is advisable to think long and hard about the right route for yourself, if necessary there are an abundance of financial advisors who would be happy to offer assistance. It is also worth noting that there is no right or wrong way; just the best method for your personal circumstances.

Standard Mortgage

Most people are familiar with the concept of a mortgage; they usually require a down payment of approximately 20%, although mortgages for investment purposes can require as much as 30%. Any borrowing is secured against the property and payments will be made monthly. The term of the loan will depend upon various criteria such as age, affordability and earnings but will usually be between ten and thirty years. Currently interest rates are very low which means you will not pay much for the funds you are being lent. However, the interest rate is variable and, if it goes up, your mortgage could cost considerably more; this should be factored into your calculations.

It is also worth considering approaching local banks as opposed to the nationwide ones; these banks may be a little more flexible in their approach and will know the local market. They can be a good option for those who do not have perfect credit ratings.

The most sensible approach if utilising this option is to follow a carefully laid out plan:

- Check your credit score. This must be the first thing you do as you will need to know which mortgage lenders are likely to be sympathetic to your needs. There are a huge number of potential lenders and many will deal with people with less than perfect credit scores. However, the better your credit score, the better the deal you will be able to get and the more profit you will be able to generate. Knowing your credit score will also give you the opportunity to correct any mistakes or issues on the report.

- Work out your budget. This will be based upon the amount of funds you have available for a deposit and the amount of capital that the lenders will provide you with. It is best, having dealt with step one, to approach one or two lenders and get an agreement in principle. This will confirm how much they are willing to lend you and how big your deposit will need to be. When arranging this it is important to consider what costs you may incur ensuring the property is up to your rental standard. If it is being purchased below market value as it needs to be modernised, you may even be able to release additional funds to assist with the work needed on the property. Since the global economic crisis there are far fewer opportunities to borrow more than a property is worth; based on what it will be worth once the repairs are completed. This does not mean there are no opportunities like this; just that you will have to look, harder for them.

- Look for your property. Now that you have a budget you will need to find a property! Use all the criteria explained later in this book to assess which is the right property for you, your budget and your current abilities.

It is important to remember that property management can be a time consuming and demanding occupation; it may be difficult to complete this properly alongside your existing responsibilities. If this is the case you will need to consider taking on a partner or property manager to ensure all repairs are completed properly.

The majority of commercial lenders will take into account all your current mortgage and debt commitments before offering a provisional mortgage; this is a mortgage which is offered subject to the right proof of income. To ensure you qualify for a mortgage you will need to have a debt to income ratio of forty three percent or less. In layman's terms this means that your total loan repayments per month, on an existing mortgage, new mortgage and even your credit cards and loans must total no more than forty three percent of you income. If you earn $1,000 per month, your borrowings will be limited to as much as you can borrow for $430 per month. The closer you are to your maximum borrowing limit the higher your interest rate is likely to be as you will be seen as a higher risk.

Whilst some lenders will take into account the rental income of a property this will depend upon whether it is immediately rentable and if it has been successfully rented in the past. If it has a very short history as a rental property it is likely the rent not be included in any calculations.

Portfolio Lenders

The majority of finance houses do not actually have the funds themselves to lend to you! They actually borrow the necessary funds from other sources; it is often the government who are the ultimate backers. In contrast, a portfolio lender is lending from their own funds. They actually own the money they are lending out. Consequentially they are able to be far more relaxed in respect of the lending criteria and the terms. They can be an excellent choice for those who are having difficulty raising funds through traditional methods. Banks do not generally advertise this type of service which can make it difficult to locate this type of lender.

This is often the only option available to people who have more than four financed properties, although there are a few lenders who will lend to investors with between four and ten properties. A portfolio lender is usually a local bank with its own capital to lend and they generally prefer to lend to local people. One of the biggest advantages of a portfolio lender is that they tend to specialize in the property market. This means they are not as strict as a commercial bank as they have a greater appreciation of what is involved in purchasing and renting property. In fact, the property you are looking to purchase does not need to be liveable; a portfolio lender will lend on potential, providing other factors, such as location, renting potential and even their personal relationship with you are all agreeable.

To ensure you get the best deal possible and that your chosen portfolio lender is happy to support you, it will be necessary to put all your accounts and finances with the local bank in question. This is a two way business deal and you should receive attractive rates on all your accounts. They want to keep you happy as you are earning them money!

To find a portfolio lender you may need to try several different routes; not everyone has even heard of a portfolio lender! One of the following steps will help you to locate a lender:

- Ask family and friends if they know one; particularly if they invest in property themselves.

- Speak to a few of your local real estate agents; they should know all the local sources of lending and be able to point you in the right direction for your needs.

- Join and attend a real estate investors group in your area. Almost every area has one; it will provide the opportunity to gather information and advice; you may be able to learn from the mistakes of others. It is highly likely that at least one of the other investors at the meetings will know a portfolio lender and can pass their details on to you.

- Your local chamber of commerce may also be able to help; they should be able to advice of which local banks are the most investor friendly.

- The internet is a great place to find almost anything! Search on portfolio lenders in your area and you should have some results. You can then call them to find which investment packages they may offer.

- Failing this you will have to go from bank to bank asking if they offer portfolio lender services. If you need to do this then it is best to target banks which are not part of a national chain.

Surprisingly, even some of the employees in a local bank may not know f they are a portfolio lender or not! If they are not sure then there are some questions you can ask them, of their lending officer to find out whether they offer portfolio lending services:

- Do they lend to property investors with four or more existing mortgages?

- Do they have a business loan or a commercial loan section, preferably based locally?

- Are your loans self-financed or do you sell them onto one of the finance houses?

- What types of loans and terms do you offer real estate investors?

- What fees do you charge for setting up a loan?

- What are your current interest rates?

- What is the maximum loan to value rate you will offer a real estate investor?

The answers to these questions will guide you as to whether they are a portfolio lender and what deals they currently offer; this information can be used to compare their facilities to other lenders in the vicinity. Finding the right portfolio lender may be a time consuming task but it is very beneficial; they will be personally interested in your endeavours and support you every step of the way!

FHA Loans

Anyone purchasing a property in the USA to live in is eligible to obtain a Federal Housing Administration loan. This is a government backed scheme to help people onto the property ladder. Instead of having to find the 20% deposit that most standard mortgage providers require, these loans can be secured with as little as a 3.5% down payment. There is one catch which is likely to make the monthly cost higher than with a traditional mortgage; you will need to take out a PMI insurance policy. This policy is a legal requirement for any secured loan under the 20% equity threshold, the cost of this insurance will increase your monthly outgoings compared to a standard mortgage but, it will place you on the property ladder and may still be cheaper than renting.

The insurance policy provides the lenders with protection from any loss occurring from the borrower defaulting on their payments. The loans can be acquired through any mainstream mortgage provider; as long as they are recognised by the FHA. There are several benefits to obtaining an FHA backed mortgage:

- The loans are offered at better rates of interest and are usually easier to take out as the requirements are lower. This is because they are insured by the government and the risk to the lender is much less than the standard mortgage.

- Your credit score needs to be over 500; this is much lower than for most mortgages. The deposit you will need to pay goes up the lower your credit score is. However, the FHA will make allowances for those without enough history to generate a fair score.

- The deposit for your purchase must be through your own funds, a gift from a family member or a government grant.

- To help with the cost of purchasing, a lender can pay the search fees, or a builder may opt to pay the closing costs. This is permissible under the FHA rules and can encourage two parties to seal the deal.

- The lender must be FHA approved, the loan does not come from the FHA; this is the insurance. It s therefore essential that they approve the lenders to ensure the customer gets a good deal. In effect taking out an FHA loan means your lender will adhere to the regulations.

- It is important to note that the insurance offered by the FHA is paid for in two parts. One part is the annual fee which is paid every month. The other part is the upfront fee; 1.75 percent of the purchase price. This amount can be added to the loan but it needs to be accounted for beforehand.

- The FHA will, in some circumstances, offer assistance when in a time of emotional hardship. This could be in the form of a delayed payment schedule, a lowering of the interest rate or even extend the period allowed for paying back the loan.

Should you wish to purchase a house which requires a substantial amount of repair or refurbishment work, it is possible to use a variation of the FHA loan; the 203K loan. This loan works along the same principles but will allow you to add the cost of these repairs to your loan; you will need a quote for the works which need doing and this may be checked by the FHA administration team. This is an incentive for people to purchase houses which would, otherwise, potentially be left to decay.

Owner Financing

Another way to finance a property purchase is to agree a finance deal with the owner of the property you wish to buy. For this arrangement to work the property must be mortgage free and there should be no secured borrowings against the house. The current owner and you could come to an agreement regarding an appropriate monthly payment; the interest charge and duration of the loan would have to be agreed. The property would not legally become yours until all payments have been made. It would be essential to have proper documents drawn up.

The key to this approach is to offer the current owner of the property an interest rate on their money that they will be hard pushed to get anywhere else. This may cost you more than a standard commercial mortgage, but there is little risk! The property remains in the name of the seller and you do not need to outlay a penny initially to get you onto the property ladder.

You must, however, be confident that you can afford the repayment to the current owner. This tactic can be a very good way to get started in real estate investing. Refinancing a house which is already yours is much easier than getting a mortgage in the first place. This approach allows you to get through the door ready to refinance in the future when your funds permit.

This can also be an appealing move to someone who is struggling to sell their property but does not need to find another one. They will establish a buyer and make a small profit on their tied-up capital without the hassle of needing to invest the money or pay tax on it. It is also possible to sell the debt onto a third party. As the buyer this would make little difference except that you pay someone else.

This type of agreement usually lasts between three and five years; this provides ample opportunity for you to refinance.

This approach is not very common as the majority of sellers are unaware that this is a possibility. It may also seem a risky proposition to a seller who may need the capital for their next purchase. However, the debt can be sold on instantly which will free the seller's money for their next house or anything else they wish to do with it. It can also be a worthwhile tactic to ensure a seller gets the full asking price; you are less likely to negotiate on the asking price if you are attempting to convince someone to allow you to buy under an owner financing arrangement.

It can also be a good way for someone who is struggling to make their mortgage payments to continue with them without losing their house or damaging their credit rating. The whole process can be completed very quickly; searches and a legal document are all that is officially required.

Hard Money

Hard money is money obtained from a business or individual who is looking to invest in real estate. A hard loan is usually for a set duration and this is not normally longer than six months. They often have much higher interest rates than a conventional loan. One advantage of this type of loan is that it does not require the usual identification and income checks; the funds can, therefore, be available very quickly – usually within a few days. All loans are based upon the value of the property and secured against it.

Another distinct advantage of this type of finance is the loan to value ratio. In many investor loans you will need a minimum of twenty percent deposit. With a hard loan this is not necessary. The value of the property is based upon what it will be worth when it has been repaired and not what it is worth now. This makes this an excellent type of finance for any property which needs to be modernised. It should be possible to borrow the entire purchase price and acquire a property without putting any funds down. Of course, it is also important to remember that most hard loans are very short term and you will need to have the property finished within that period if you hope to return the investment from the proceeds of the sale.

The easiest way to find a hard loan lender is to look on the internet; they should provide a guide to their rates and charges to help you compare them with any other options. Some lenders are only able to do it within their state whilst others can do it nationwide. This does not affect the service that they can offer

Another type of loan which is similar in context to hard money is 'private money'. It is likely that funds sought this way will also be short term, but the funds will be made available by someone who is not currently registered as a loan provider; this means they are likely to be either a member of your family or a close friend. Care should be taken when dealing with family or friends as money can easily sour a good relationship.

In fact a private lender can mend to anyone they choose; but, it may be extremely difficult to convince someone you do not know that you would be a good risk for their funds. This is why private lenders tend to be close family and friends; they need to be able to trust the person they are lending to. It is possible to secure the funds from a source such as this; you may find someone advertising on the web.

Unfortunately, many of the companies which advertise on the internet will charge you a fee and then simply hook you up with a hard money lender.

Perhaps the best way to secure private money is to ask your friends and family who is known to be wealthy in your home town. Then approach them with a good business plan in a professional manner. You may need to offer them a share of the profits or some other incentive to close the deal. Perhaps one of the greatest things about a private lender is that you are able to discuss a proposed deal and adjust it to a mutually agreeable solution.

Although many lenders may prefer to lend to family and friends, there are those that will see your project as a drop in their financial wealth; thereby justifying the risk and doing a little good at the same time.

Home Equity Loans

This method is only of use to those who have already purchased a home and have been living in it for at several years. This should be sufficient time to build up some equity in your current property and there are many lenders who will release this equity for you. One advantage of this funding method is that you are able to purchase a property that the bank may not approve of. This is often true of properties which need major repair works; the bank is simply concerned with whether you can afford the repayments and whether there is enough equity in your house; they are not concerned with what you are using the funds for.

This type of financing can be used to raise a deposit before purchasing a second or even third property. However, under the 43% debt to income rules which were described in then standard mortgage section, the additional borrowing on your home loan will affect your ability to borrow more funds against another property. In truth borrowing from your own home to finance another purchase is a difficult option unless you have owned you home for a long period of time and have a large amount of equity in it. Using this equity as a deposit will allow you to borrow the rest of the money under a standard mortgage and effectively have purchased an investment property for no cash outlay. Of course, you will have increased your debt undertaking and your risk of disaster if it all goes wrong.

It is also possible to set up a home equity credit line. This will provide you with instant access to an agreed amount of equity in your property, when you want it. Unlike a loan you can take a little or all the amount when it suits you; this prevents you from making loan repayments in money that has been approved but not yet used.

Whilst this can be a more straight forward way to purchase an investment property you must remember that your home is secured against it; fail to pay and you could lose it.

Equity Partnership

Should you be unable to locate sufficient funds through any of the above methods then it may be possible to find an equity partner. A partner will provide the funds needed for either the purchase of the property or the deposit needed. Once the property is purchased an equity partner may wish to have an active role in the development and management of it; equally, they may prefer to sit back and wait for you to provide them with a return on their investment. Equity partners do not normally receive any interest on their investment; their return comes from the profit made by either renting or selling the property. This makes it a riskier proposition than some other forms of lending.

The internet is full of companies which will offer their services as an equity partner. It is important to read their terms and conditions before going ahead with any of them. Choosing the right partner is about more than just the best rate; they should be there to support you and assist you in achieving your goal. If you pick the wrong partner they will simply shut you down at the first sign of trouble.

There are several factors to take into account when choosing an equity partner:

- Analyse the property you would like to purchase. Its location, size, intended use and its price will all affect the type of equity partners who will be interested in helping you. An equity partner can be a big firm which deals with large scale investments and may not be interested in one particular property or an individual investor who would rather deal with one property and dedicate their efforts to helping you.

- Once you have selected several equity partners who should be interested in the size of the deal you are hoping for you will need to contact them. It is best to arrange a face to face meeting so that you can explain your intentions and show your business plan. The more prepared and professional you are the easier it will be for someone to say yes.

Having presented your project to several equity partners you will, hopefully, be made an offer by more than one of them! This means you will need to select the right one for you and your project. It is worth checking your potential partners for the following:

- How much experience do they have? The more experience, the more they should be able to assist you in making decisions and, perhaps more importantly, they will understand the property market and will not reacting badly instantly to something which does not go to plan. Instead their experience will allow them to guide you through it.

- Funds – If your equity partner has all their funds tied up in your project they will become very anxious and liable to pressure you to ensure the profit is made quickly; even if this is not a realistic option. They may also be unable to provide additional capital if an unforeseen issue arises. Ideally the firm you choose should have the capital needed for your project and have a multitude of other projects of similar size of bigger on the go; this will keep the pressure off you and allow you to get the job done.

- Your equity partner will need to sign off on several things throughout your project. This means you should be able to sit down with them and discuss things rationally and fairly. They should be able to assist you in seeing all sides of the issue and, together, come to an agreeable solution. Experience plays a part in this, but an ability to connect with the other person is vital.

Commercial Credit

If you are purchasing a property with the sole aim of renting it, developing it or flipping it then there are many commercial lenders who may be prepared to lend you the necessary funds. These lenders will view your proposition as a business and not as a property purchase; they will be interested in the income potential of the building and the expected profit margins. Rates of interest can be extremely low when borrowing commercially and the lender has little interest in the credit worthiness of the customer. This can be an excellent method to secure funds for bigger projects, as a commercial lender will look at the bigger picture.

As a rule a commercial credit option is only available if you are a company. If this is your first real estate purchase you are unlikely to want to form a company and this option may not be the best for you. If, however, you already have several properties and are looking to expand them then this could be the perfect solution.

A commercial credit lender will look at all your properties as income streams, the total income from all of these should be more than the total expenditure. Providing there is enough left to cover a loan payment you have a good chance of being approved for a loan. They may ask for a personal guarantee; this is when you will personally pay back the money, even if your company goes into liquidation.

If you are running your real estate investments as a business and building a portfolio it can be very useful to develop a good relationship with a commercial credit provider. As already mentioned, they are lending to your business and will base their decision in the profitability if the business. The funds can be used to purchase more properties, or they can be used to assist with the day to day running of the business. A company which understands the real estate market will be best positioned to help through the ups and downs of the market and the economy in general.

To approach a commercial credit group you will need to have both a profit and loss statement for your company and a balance sheet. Ideally you will have these for the last three years. If your business is younger than this then it is advisable to include some cash flow forecasts and a statement of intention regarding your purchasing schedules.

The profit and loss will show your income received from all your properties and the expenditure which has been needed to keep the properties going; this may include management fees, insurance, repairs, rates and even improvement costs.

In contrast the balance sheet will show all the assets you own and all the liabilities you owe; such as finance or unpaid supplier bills. Depreciation should also be shown and the figure at the bottom will show the business's net worth.

Subject To

This technique has been around for many years. In essence you are simply taking over the property from the current owner. There is a clause in almost every mortgage contract which prevents this, normally a property cannot be transferred unless the outstanding mortgage is settled. However, as interest rates are so low at the moment, and have been for some time, there is little benefit to the banks enforcing this clause. As such, unless you cause them a lot of extra work they will not notice or worry about a transfer of ownership.

To purchase a property via the 'subject to' method requires you to convince the current owner to pass the deed of ownership over to you but retain the mortgage debt themselves. In return you will agree to pay the monthly mortgage amount, and will want to because if you do not you will lose the property. You can make an arrangement directly with the seller or you can arrange to make the payments through an intermediary; if this provides them with peace of mind.

This technique is very successful when dealing with someone who is under threat of foreclosure. By taking in the property and the mortgage repayments you are preserving the seller's credit rating, and gaining yourself another property. Of course, for this to be an effective solution the seller will need to have little or no equity in the property and you will probably need to agree upon a timescale when you pay them off in full; possibly through refinancing.

If you take this approach it is important to make sure you deal with the insurance properly and effectively. You will need to either be added to the homeowner's current policy; then follow up in a couple of weeks by changing it to a 'renters' policy. Alternatively you can cancel the policy and take out a new one in joint names or even take your own policy out separately.

Seller Second

This option is useful if you do not have enough capital available to purchase the real estate property you want. Assuming you have a deposit you will have approached a mortgage lender and agreed a deal. However, if the mortgage lender is not prepared to lend you the rest of the money you may end up with a shortfall. The mortgage lender is obviously expecting you to find the extra capital.

Providing you are convinced that the property can be improved and worth considerably more and that the rent charged will warranty the additional cost, it is possible to get a second mortgage on the property. The primary mortgage is known as the first position; they will be the first one to receive funds if the property has to be resold. To make up the difference the seller will have to agree to take out a second mortgage on the property; which will be legally paid by the borrower. This mortgage is known as a 'sellers second' and they will be second in line to the funds if the property has to be sold.

It is not possible to take out a 'sellers second' without the permission of the first position lender. This is because it will increase the risk and exposure of both lenders. The new owner may have very little capital invested in the property and is, therefore, at higher risk of defaulting.

The terms of the second mortgage must be agreed in a legal contract between you and the seller to ensure they are not liable for any costs further down the line. The interest rate is likely to be higher in this loan than the primary mortgage as this loan is at a higher risk. You will need to pay the seller the agreed amount each month for the term of the loan; usually five years.

Lease Option

If you are desperate to get into the real estate market but have been unable to secure funding so far, it may be possible for you to buy through a lease option. This is a good idea if you are very young with no real credit history or have bad credit.

This option provides you the right to move into a house for a set period of time and to rent the property for that time period. At the end of the period you have the right to buy the property at the price you agreed at the start of the lease. A lease will usually last for between six months and two years. After this you either purchase the house or move out.

Before opting for a lease option you should consider the following:

- There is an upfront fee which puts the right to buy into a contract form; making it legally binding. This is usually the equivalent of two month's rent. Can you afford this?

- Lease options tend to cost more than straight forward renting; before you commit to one make sure you are happy to stay in the area for at least the duration of the lease, if not much longer.

- If you are unable to secure a mortgage now or alternative finance, are you sure you will be able to by the time the lease ends?

- Can you afford the monthly lease payments and all the other bills which come with the property?

If you are sure this is the route for you then you will need to locate either a house that is offering this scheme or attempt to convince a seller that this is a good deal for them. You will need a lawyer to help you negotiate the terms of the lease.

This is a good option for those who have poor credit as it provides them with their dream home and enough time to rebuild their credit rating. It can also be a useful tool to getting another property in your investment portfolio when the majority of your existing capital is already in use.

Wholesaling Real Estate

This approach to real estate investing requires very little funds on your part and will provide you with the opportunity to learn a lot about the real estate investment business. It should also provide you with the opportunity to build your own capital to enable you to purchase a property through the more traditional channels.

Wholesale real estate is the process of buying a property and whilst the property purchase is going through assigning the contract to another party. In effect, you will need to find a property cheap enough than you can mark it up slightly, without doing anything to it. The new price must be attractive enough that someone else will still be able to buy it and make a profit.

In effect you are selling the property before it is actually yours; in some states this practice is not allowed so check carefully before you undertake this option. You will need to be able to get a mortgage capable of buying a property although you will never actually complete on the mortgage as the person you have assigned the contract to will provide the funds for you.

The key to success with this approach is finding properties cheap enough that other investors will be willing to buy them off you; after you have made your profit. This is not a scheme which will enable you to make a lot of money on each sale, but it will give you an insight into the industry and allow you to build sufficient funds to purchase your own property in the future.

To locate the right properties you may need to create your own marketing campaign and keep your eyes peeled at all times. Buying property at low prices is a very competitive field and you often need to be extremely quick to seal any prospective deal.

Non Performing Notes

This approach is a way into real estate investment but it does require you to either have capital available or have a third party ready to back you. In the past if someone was unable to meet their mortgage repayments the mortgage company would foreclose and auction off the property. However, this incurs more time and costs, mortgage companies have now adopted a new approach. They will sell the mortgage debt, known as a 'Non Performing Note'. As the loan is not performing it is sold at a significant discount. You are then left with the loan, secured on a property and the homeowner must pay you.

You will then have several options; you can deal with the current homeowner and negotiate better payment terms for them; this will return your capital over time with interest. Alternatively you can foreclose on the property and then choose to sell it or rent it out. As the non performing note has been purchased at a hefty discount there is plenty of room to make a healthy profit; although you will have to deal with the costs of foreclosing.

This practice has happened for years but the non performing loans are usually sold en mass and are only available to other financial institutions. It is only recently that it has become possible to purchase an individual non performing note and invest in the real estate market this way.

There are many businesses which can help you to perform a loan modification or foreclosure but be mindful that their charges will eat into your profit. Before you purchase this type of real estate you must check exactly what you are buying and whether there are any taxes or dues which you may become liable for. It is a complex area of real estate but also has a lot of potential, if you can deal with evicting people from their homes.

There will always be other options for obtaining finance for your investment purchase; perhaps the most important advice is to stick at it until you obtain the necessary funds. It may even be worth trying crowd funding!

It is important to consider the additional expenses when planning your investment property purchase. There will be legal fee involved in the purchase and possible some maintenance required; even on a ready to rent property. Alongside this there will be the usual expenses; utility bills, maintenance, insurance and potentially management fees. Before committing to any project you should be aware of the expected costs and have enough funds available to cover them. It is also a good idea to have a little extra in reserve to deal with unexpected issues; this will ensure you investment does not collapse at the first hurdle.

Chapter 2 – The Right Investment Type

There are two main types of investment; income earning and non-income earning. Any property which is purchased to live in, used as a holiday home or is currently vacant can be described as a non-income earning property. It is possible to make funds on this type of property but this is reliant on the property going up in value. Property development falls in to this category as the usual process is to buy either a piece of land or a property in need of repair (usually an apartment block or something similar). The purchase is then developed into something which can be sold and a profit made.

Flipping houses is also a form of non-income earning investment; this involves the purchase of a property and redecorating or modifying it to increase its value before selling it on again. This type of real estate investment requires a good knowledge of the property market and current prices. You will also need to be aware of the cost of hiring contractors to repair and renovate; it is not usually a practical option to do these activities yourself. You then need to find properties at a suitably low price and complete the work before putting it back on the market at a much higher price as quickly as possible.

There are four different types of Income earning investments, these are as follows:

- **Residential**

Buying a property specifically to lease it to someone for them to live in is a form of income producing investment. There are many different types of property available on the market which would fall into this category. You may wish to purchase a family home and rent it to a family, or it can be rented as rooms to a variety of people with a shared living space. Equally you could purchase a block of apartments and rent each of the apartments to a tenant, this can potentially generate a high return on investment. Another option is to purchase a house and divide it into two apartments; these can then be rented separately. The option you choose will depend upon the capital you have available, the properties in your area and the demand for property.

- **Office**

As the name suggests this is the purchase of office space which is then rented to a business for long term use. Business leases tend to be long term which means that once you have a reliable tenant you are unlikely to need to worry about your investment for some time. The increase in technology and the reliance that everyone has on this technology has meant an increase in the number of businesses which need an office space. This is excellent news for the property investor who has a number of offices in their portfolio or is looking to purchase more. Office investment should be approached with a little caution as it is one of the first casualties when the economy has a downturn. Despite the long term leases which are usually created, a company can go into liquidation over night leaving you with no one to pay the rent. This can be made worse if you find that you have not held the company owner personally liable and you have no possibility of obtaining any funds owed.

- **Retail**

Most cities have at least one shopping mall and a variety of shops on the high street. Even small towns and villages have a range of shops, cafes and restaurants. Not every business owner can afford to purchase their property, particularly when first setting up their business. This means that there is an excellent market for businesses wishing to lease a property. A lease will be set up for a guaranteed length of time and a set rate with pre-established times when the rent may be reviewed. This means that an investor has a degree of security once the property has been leased to a business. You should be looking for either one property or a group of properties; investors with a large amount of financial backing would choose to purchase the entire mall.

It is often advisable to look for a 'big' retail shop, such as a big supermarket chain or clothing shop. These well known brands will attract customers to the area and this means that any shop nearby can count on a good flow of potential customers. Shops purchased near these 'big' stores will be easier to rent to businesses; you may even be able to attract your tenant to you simply by advertising the proximity of the 'big' retailer. Businesses which produce complimentary products to the 'big' retailer will be eager to occupy your premises.

- **Industrial**

Most industrial properties are cheaper to purchase than a corresponding residential, office or retail investment. This is because the average industrial unit is completely unfurnished and only has power and water going to it. Businesses prefer units like this as they are able to set the area up for their own requirements; this is usually cheaper than attempting to adapt an existing set-up.

In addition most industrial units have very low operating costs and need little time management, most businesses prefer to be left to get on with it their own way. This makes industrial property investment an attractive option for the first time investor. It is possible to provide a lease which leaves you liable for all maintenance and modification costs; care should be used if purchasing a property with a lease like this already in place.

Location does play a part when looking to purchase an investment industrial unit. It must be easily accessible for a truck and relatively close to a good road network, rail or even shipping channels. It is also essential to confirm that a prospective building has adequate height clearance for forklifts or other machinery which a business may wish to use.

The Decision

It is essential to consider the pros and cons of each of these types of investment, some properties are more suited to one type of investor than others. You should consider the following before committing to any specific type of real estate investment:

- Budget

This is possibly the biggest part of any investment decision! You must look at which properties you can afford and then decide which of these are the most likely to provide good returns. If your funds will allow you to purchase a house in a bad area of town or an industrial unit in a good location; the industrial unit should be a clear winner.

- Management

Any property will require managing, this may be the yearly maintenance and insurance or it may involve looking after the tenants and sourcing new ones periodically. If you intend to manage the property yourself you must make sure you know the demands it will place on your time and your finances. The different types of property will place different demands and this may influence your decision.

- Location

It is essential to purchase a property in the right location. As mentioned an industrial unit should be near good access routes; a retail unit should be near a 'big' store and an office should be in the same district as other offices. Residential properties vary according to the type of tenant you are trying to attract. Students will need to be near the university, business workers will want to be near the business sector and families will want to be near the good schools and close to all amenities. Before committing to an investment property; make sure it is in the right location!

- Goals

You may be purchasing just one investment property or you may be looking to start an empire of your own. It is essential to know what you are aiming for and to develop a plan of how you will get there. Whilst there will always be set backs along the way; having a plan will ensure you know where you are going and what you need to do to get there. Part of this plan will involve deciding which type of investment is right for you and purchasing that, regardless of what other attractive offers may appear.

- Spread the risk

The best portfolios have a mix of property types; this is the most effective way to insulate against market downturns. Always study the current market to establish the best type of property to purchase next; the larger your portfolio the more stable it will be.

- Finance

Before you can choose any property type you should already have looked at the different types of finance, decided on the one that suits you the most and made provisional arrangements. This means you will know what your budget is and any other terms which may apply; this is essential to ensure you choose a property you can afford!

- Rental market

It is important to consider whether the area you are purchasing in has a large amount of renters or more owners. Owner occupied, whether business or residential, tend to be less tolerant of landlords. They are also likely to be situated in a part of town that is unaffordable to the majority of renters and this will seriously limit your potential tenants and, therefore, income.

- Know your market

As soon as you commit to the idea of property investment you should start to learn everything about the market that you can. This is also the time to start networking and building a list of useful contacts; these may be invaluable in the future for either emergency funding or advice.

Chapter 3 – Choosing the Right Property

Deciding to invest in real estate is only the first step, although it may be the biggest! Once you have committed to investing and building your portfolio there are a lot of issues to deal with; from choosing the investment type to arrange finance and possibly even locating tenants.

However, no matter which investment type you wish to attempt first you will need to choose a property. This is when it is especially important to remember that real estate investing is a business; you cannot choose a property because it is beautiful or you have fallen in love with it! There is a set of criteria by which any property can be judged and you can impartially assess whether it will make a worthwhile investment property:

The One Percent Rule

A general rule to stick to is the one percent rule. You must work out what rent you will be able to reasonable collect on a given property. When you are new to the real estate industry you may not be aware of the likely rental value if a given property; if this is the case it is best to speak to some local letting agents. They should be able to advise you of what sort of price is fair for the property you are looking at. If they think you are considering using their services to manage the property they will be eager to help!

The rental value should be at least one percent of the total purchase cost of your property. For instance, if you were looking at a property which would cost you $100,000 the rent should be at least $1,000 per month. If the rental income is likely to be lower than this it is best to walk away and locate a different policy. It is also important to note that the cost is not just the price of the property; it should include purchasing costs and the cost of any work you know needs doing.

There are people that you are safer if you aim for two percent, but this may mean that you miss out on a host of perfectly acceptable deals. However, if the property is in a higher risk area then you may prefer to opt for a higher percent rule; to safeguard your investment.

The safest properties and ones which are definitely in the one percent rule are those in desirable neighbourhoods, turnover of tenants is low and very few houses are unoccupied for any length of time. These types of property attract affluent tenants who demand the best locations and enjoy luxury lifestyles. The one percent rule remains a safe bet as you move into the middle class tenant; people who earn a respectable income, still wish to live in a good area but are restricted by budget. These tenants tend to occupy slightly older houses which may need a little work doing on them from time to time.

You will need to move to a two percent rule when faced with properties in 'danger zones'. These are areas which have a high turnover of tenants, high crime rates and poor quality housing. Tenants in these houses tend to be on a lower income. It is possible to find areas even worse than this any you may need to consider a three percent rule; if you are brave enough to be a landlord in these areas.

The one percent rule is a loose guide to the rate of return you are likely to get on your investment; it is not definitive. In principle, it works like this:

- Rate of return of 1% equals a 12% return on the year.

- Average maintenance, repairs and management fees take 50% of your income. This can vary as some years there will be little or no repairs whilst other years will see huge bills. Research suggests that, on average, the 50% rule is accurate.

- Your rate of return is halved by these costs so equals 6%

- Property, on average, appreciates by 3% each year; again this is a variable figure but this is a good average.

- Actual rate of return equals 6% + 3%: 9%

The average investor on the stock market receives between seven and nine percent, again this is a variable figure but it is a good guideline. Following the one percent rule will give you a likely return the same as the top end of investing in the stock market. If you go below this rule then you may as well invest your funds in the stock market and collect your interest every year; you will be no worse off and have encountered a lot less hassle.

Cashflow Return

The rate of return deals with your likely return from your investment; however, there is another factor to consider. The rate of return on your cashflow is a good guide as to whether a property is a worthwhile investment or not as if the rate is low you will get better returns by investing your capital elsewhere. To calculate the cashflow return rate, follow these steps:

- Work out the rent possible for the year: i.e. $1,200 per month equals $14,400 per year.

- Add any other income, if there is any, such as a cleaning fee.

- The figure you end up with is your gross operating income.

- Add up your overheads and remove them from your gross operating income. This is the maintenance costs, utility bills and management fees. For this example let's say this is $500 per month or $6,000 per year.

- Net operating income equals $14,400 - $6,000: $8,400

- Simply divide this figure by the total cost price (including purchase costs and initial repairs) and multiply by 100 to obtain a percentage figure: If the cost price was $100,000 then it would be 8.4%

- This is a reasonable rate of return and one worth considering. You will need to set your own parameters but generally anything below 7% is not considered worthwhile as you can get a better rate of return on your cashflow elsewhere.

After you have decided if the house is financially viable you will need to consider some other factors:

The Neighbourhood

The one percent rule will help you regarding which neighbourhoods are most likely to qualify financially. However, there are instances where this is not completely applicable. You are best to visit a neighbourhood at various times of the day and different days of the week; this is the best way to ensure it is as good as it first appears. Many neighbourhoods can appear quiet and tranquil in the daytime when the children are at school and the parents are at work. It can be a different story when they all come home! The real estate agent may not want to advise you on the late night activities as they are interested in selling the property. You must do your own research.

Another good indication, when looking around a neighbourhood, is the number of properties on the market. If there are a lot, particularly close together, you must ask what do they know that you don't.

The type of neighbourhood can also affect your income, property near a university will be difficult to rent in the summer holiday time.

Property Taxes

Everyone has to pay a property tax but they are the same across any city. The rates are decided by the local government and it is possible to check with the assessment office in the town and it is a good idea to do so. People may be put off renting if the taxes are high, even if your rent is cheap; they may still get a better deal in a more expensive neighbourhood!

Local Amenities

Many tenants will look into the neighbourhood before deciding on whether to rent a property or not. They may wish to be near good travel links, or near a good school; they may simply prefer to be within walking distance of some good shops. You may not be able to cater for everyone's tastes bit you must consider which amenities are near your investment property and the quality if these amenities. It may be helpful to look at the tourist summary for the city or district; they will usually provide a guide to the facilities in any given area and this can be useful information to help you make a decision.

Crime Rates

You will need to visit either the police or the public library to find out the most accurate information regarding crime rates in specific neighbourhoods. This is essential as even a well looked after neighbourhood can have a high crime rate. If your tenants do not feel safe in the property they will move on and you will be left with the costs of finding new tenants and a lack of income from repeat vacancies. For this reason it is essential to choose a property in a low crime area.

Jobs

Tenants need jobs if they are to continue paying you rent! Choosing an area which is undergoing a growth in employment possibilities is likely to make it attractive to potential tenants. This will mean an influx of people to an area and will make it much easier for you to rent your property.

Future Developments

You should check with the local planning department regarding any new builds or developments which are planned for an area. A large amount of property construction will suggest that it is a good area for you to buy in; although this will increase the competition and may make it harder for you to attract a tenant.

New developments can also destroy existing community spaces and create bad feeling in a neighbourhood; it is important to assess the impact of any development on the neighbourhood before you make a decision on the property. The best rule to follow when considering developments is if you would be happy with the development you will probably be able to find tenants to live in your property. If you wouldn't be happy, walk away!

Natural Disasters

You cannot control what Mother Nature will do to the area you are thinking of investing in, but you can look at past experiences to assess the likely affect on insurance costs in a specific area. The more likely it is to have a natural disaster the higher the insurance cost and the lower your profits will be.

Type of property

As a general rule the best tenants are families; this is because they generally seek stability and are looking for long term rentals. Purchasing a family dwelling will attract families and couples; it is highly unlikely that a single person will want to rent a family home. Couples and families generally have two incomes which makes them more likely to be able to afford the rent, even if one of them experiences financial difficulties.

Appreciation Potential

Some of the best properties are those which can be bought for less than the market value and need a small amount of work doing to them. It should be possible to renovate the property and then charge the top rate for the neighbourhood. A well renovated house in the right neighbourhood will attract the best tenants and will have the added benefit of adding value to your investment through both the appreciation of the housing market and the improvements to your property.

As part of this it is important to research on the internet and speak to those who have sold property in the area; this will provide you with a guide to the real value of property in the area; it is often sold for less than the advertised price. You do not want to think you have a good price for a property, when, in fact, you have paid the average going rate.

Data

An additional source of data regarding the performance of property in specific locations and the amount of defaults in an area can be found by contacting the lenders and insurers. The data will be generalised but will indicate any obvious trends.

The Decor

This is an important aspect of any property. The easiest property to rent is one which has been painted in neutral colours. If you are viewing properties which do not fit this bill you will need to consider the time and cost involved in redecorating the property. This may not be enough of an issue to justify a price drop and could create a dent in your profits before you even start. However, a well presented property will attract a better tenant and allow you to charge the maximum rent for the area. An additional factor in the decor is the standard of the kitchen and the bathroom. These must be modern and well presented to ensure your tenants will be comfortable in their new home.

The Cost

The various sums illustrated will summarize whether the property is likely to make a good rate of return and be a sensible investment opportunity. However, this is not the same as being able to afford a property. Even if the property stacks up and you can arrange finance through one of the financing routes discussed, it may still not be the right option for you. Property investment can be stressful, there are no guarantees and an economical slowdown can quickly place you in an untenable situation. Before committing to purchase a real estate investment you must be comfortable that you can afford it and it will not place an undue strain on you, your family and your finances. Investing for the future is an admirable goal, but it should never be at the cost of your quality of life today; you must find an investment property which will balance all the different factors; even if it takes a lengthy amount of time to find the right property for your needs.

Income

It is important to remember that a real estate investment is all about the income you can and will make. In the past investors have been obsessed with the idea that property will rise in value and they can make their money by selling it in a few years. It was this type of investor who got the most badly burnt during the economic recession. The reason for this is that they bought because they could get finance, but the moment that they could no longer sell for a profit they fell into negative equity and their debts were simply too high to recover from.

In contrast, if you stick to the income potential of a property and see any appreciation as an added bonus you will keep your borrowing to more affordable levels. This does not mean that an economic downturn could not have a serious affect on your income, but, if you have bought for the right reasons, you should see an increase in potential tenants and, even if your income drops you will be able to earn enough to keep your investments afloat. Buying property for the income it can generate will not protect you from a recession but it will put you in a much stronger position to survive one. If you always look at the worst possible scenario then you will be prepared for anything.

Litigation

If you are considering buying a property inside an apartment block you will need to do some research on the state of the Home Owners Association. This is an association which is formed by the developer of a property, its aim is to manage the marketing and sale of the apartments as well as managing the building itself. An association allows the developer to distant themselves from the building financially; it usually becomes a separate corporation of its own once a certain number of apartments have been sold.

As a buyer you will have no choice but to become part of the HOA; it is therefore essential to research the HOA first to ensure it is financially secure and is not facing any litigation cases. If has issues with either of these you may find your property ownership becomes messy and expensive; it is better to walk away while you can.

Standards

A rentable home must conform to certain regulations and standards. These are subject to change from time to time and it essential to stay up to date with the latest set of regulations. You will need to check with the landlord and tenant laws which apply to your specific state to confirm the exact standards which you must conform to.

This s an important consideration as you may need to fit handrails on the entrances to the front and back doors, reinforced doors, a peephole in the front door, deadlocks and even a dividing wall being a fire wall. The cost of the items on this short list will come to over $3,000 and may seriously affect your sums; particularly if you were not prepared for them. It is essential to check the code for your area and ensure that either your intended property has the necessary items to conform to the code or that you know how much they will cost to fix; this will ensure you factor them into your equations.

As you can now see there are many factors which should be considered before you start investing in the real estate market. This may make the whole scenario seem complicated and confusing, in fact, if you follow the advice her and take your time doing your preparation work you will be able to find a property which suits your needs and returns you a good profit. Of course there will be difficult times and exceptionally good times; being prepared means that you will be in the best position possible to weather any storm and remain in real estate investment for as long as you like.

Whether your ultimate aim is to pass your properties onto your heirs, free of any mortgage or debt, or whether you are intending to sell them all in the future and retire on the money generated, it is essential to look after your properties and your tenants. This will put you in the best position if or when you decide to sell.

One final point that should be noted is that it is possible to purchase a property which already has a tenant in it. This makes it much easier to perform your calculations regarding viability of the property. It also eliminates the need to find a tenant. However, you should assess the contract carefully as you do not want to purchase the property and then be locked into a lease agreement which cannot be changed as is heavily in the favour of your new tenant!

Chapter 4 – Building Your Real estate Passive Income

Many people dream of leaving the daily grind and enjoying the good life. Property investment can make this is reality but it is not an easy path and does require a large amount of commitment and a lot of hard work. A passive income is generated once you have purchased enough property that you can enjoy a good standard of living from the income, after allowing for all necessary expenditures, including taxes. If you are starting from scratch it is imperative to draw up a plan and follow it; at the same time you must be open and flexible to whatever opportunities come your way.

The following guide will assist you with building a property empire, from which you can enjoy a passive income:

- **Building your money**

Before you can build your empire you need to have some funds; it is incredibly difficult to purchase any property without capital. The more funds you are able to input into your first purchase the stronger your financial position will be. However, there is no point in putting off starting your empire until you have sufficient funds available; unless you have a plan to raise these funds and you are able to stick to your plan. If you choose this route then the funds should be available within two years; if this is not possible it is unlikely that your real estate empire will ever become more than an ambition. There is a point at which you must recognize it is better to get started on building your passive income; saving your initial down payment can take too much time.

In order to get started in real estate you will need to choose one of the finance methods already described. There are options available which will require minimal funding from your own pocket although this may mean that you need a business partner.

- **Choosing a route**

Having saved and secured some funding you will now need to draw up a plan as to which type of property you wish to purchase. A balanced portfolio will have a little of each of the main types; this will help to spread the risk and improve your position during any economic downturn.

Part of choosing your route will involve drawing up a plan regarding how many properties you would like to own in total and how often you will purchase a property. The plan should also include where the funding will come from and a breakdown of the purchase costs, expenses and expected income.

- **Property Prices**

The price of property can vary significantly depending upon the time of property and the location of the property. Before purchasing your first property you must assess the most viable option; the cheapest properties on the market are not always the best! If the property you purchase requires work then this must be factored into your plans and your budgets; it will take more time to complete these improvements before you are able to start receiving any income.

Equally, a property which has just been refurbished and is ready to rent may not be the best purchase if it is not in the right location. Or, the rent which would be required to cover the mortgage and other costs is far higher than other properties in that area rent for.

Before purchasing it is essential to understand the market, what is a fair price and which properties are likely to be in demand with tenants.

- **Choosing when to flip or hold**

The aim of purchasing property is that it will create a passive income for you. Your income is the amount of rent received less any running costs, including your finance charges; however, owning one property should provide you with a small income; but it will not b enough for you to leave your current job! To generate a passive income which will allow you to quit your day job you will need to purchase multiple properties; the exact number should be worked out in your plan.

There are a great many properties on the market which can be purchased at a price lower than market value; these properties usually require work to bring them back to a good standard. Buying below market value can be an excellent way of improving your profit margins, however; it is essential to understand the costs involved in repairing the property. If you do not work out these costs then you can quickly spend more on your cheap house than it would cost to purchase one which is already refurbished.

Once you have refurbished the property you must decide whether to flip it (sell it on), preferably at a profit; or whether to keep it and rent it. Whilst the ultimate aim is to own enough properties to create a good standard of living for yourself through rental income, it is imperative to realise that flipping can be a good way of raising the funds needed to purchase more properties.

Flipping a property can be hard work, particularly if you decide to undertake the work yourself; this is not advisable unless you are a qualified builder. Doing it yourself will be likely to take too much of your time and the project will take much longer to complete. You will need to develop a relationship with a local building firm that you can trust; they can take care of the refurbishment. Knowing exactly when to flip and when to keep your latest property can be a difficult decision; you must consider the current state of the market and how much profit you can make from the sale. Flipping houses can be an excellent way to build up your own capital; this will allow you to purchase more properties and create a better cushion against market changes.

- **Understanding the financial implications**

Every purchase has a range of costs which are associated with it. Property purchases usually involve relatively costly legal fees as well as, potentially, commission due to the real estate agent. Even if you do not need to put funds aside to cover the cost of refurbishment you must be aware of the bills that your property will incur. These include insurance costs, maintenance costs and marketing fees. Alongside this you will almost certainly need to employ the services of a management agency; this will cost, it is usually charged as a percentage of the rent. These figures should be included in your initial calculations to ensure you will actually make money from the project.

- **Finding and looking after tenants**

As you build your real estate portfolio you will not have the time to spare to manage each property; it is highly likely that you will need the services of a management company. A management company will advertise for tenants and verify any prospective tenants suitability; including their ability to pay the rent. They will be the first point of contact and will deal with all issues at the property; if necessary contacting you first. Many of the property management companies also offer guarantees that they will keep your property rented or they will pay you the rent themselves.

When choosing a property management company it is imperative to discuss them with other investors, this is the public face of your business and you need them to be active when searching for tenants; they should always offer a first class service to your tenants.

- **Reaching your goal**

Your business plan will have established when you expect to have purchased enough houses to generate the passive income you desire. However, upon reaching that goal and being able to quit your current job you will need to evaluate your position and how it can be improved upon. One of the most important factors which should be looked at is the amount of borrowing you have; the less you have the safer and stronger your position is; regardless of economic influences.

Once you have the number of properties you require you will need to establish a new plan; this may be to continue to increase your portfolio or it may be simply to retire and enjoy it!

- **The future**

Once you have purchased enough properties to create a good passive income you are free to look at what options are available to you. One part of any plan should look at the feasibility of clearing all finance on your properties; this should be the ultimate goal of any property investor. Without any outstanding finance you will greatly increase your turnover, profit margin and your economic position. Continuing to flip houses is one proven method of generating the necessary funds to pay off the other financial commitments.

Once you have established and followed your plan you will build a portfolio of houses and these will create a passive income. This will leave you free to enjoy life and pursue other activities. With a steady income secured it can be a wonderful opportunity to look at other activities which interest you; such as skiing or starting your own business.

Chapter 5 – The World of Property Development

It is possible to deal in the world of real estate without having to deal with tenants. Property development is a type of non-earning income which can be exceptionally lucrative, although it comes with a high amount of risk. People who have been investing in the real estate market for years may still enjoy the additional excitement of developing property; for those that are new to investing in real estate the world of property development can be an excellent tool for creating their own capital.

The term property development applies to purchasing land and building property on it, or, purchasing an extremely dilapidated building and either knocking it down and starting again or restoring it. Having developed the property the aim is either to sell the new building or buildings on and make a good return on your investment or to keep the property and rent it to suitable tenants. The decision as to which option suits your needs will be based upon how you financed the purchase of the development site and whether you need the funds for another project. Property development is often funded by short term commercial loans and the properties will need to be sold to cover the cost of the loan; the profit from the real estate development can be ploughed into another development. If you have already established a reasonable real estate empire and have not got significant borrowings against your development project, it may be advisable to keep the building and increase your passive income by renting out the apartments or property as a whole.

Before starting any property development project it is essential to read and follow these guidelines:

- **Education – Theory and Practice**

One of the most important parts of real estate development is, understanding the theory that goes behind building any project. You may not need in-depth knowledge of every aspect of building but you do need to understand the terms; this will ensure you can converse professionally with anyone involved in your project. It is possible to enrol in a course which is specifically designed for property developers.

Alongside understanding the theory it is essential to talk to people who have or are developing property. These people will provide a wealth of information which is not available on any course; you can learn a huge amount from their experiences and avoid making the same mistakes.

- **Building Sites**

The next step is to look at prospective building sites. As already mentioned you have the option of looking at buildings which need knocking down or a plot of land which can be built on. If you choose an existing site it is highly unlikely there will be any issue with you building there; although you will still need to seek permission from the local government. You should also be aware that they may insist on you keeping some or all of the original features of the building you are about to demolish. This can make it very difficult to create the building you have designed and can, potentially, add significant additional costs to your project.

Locating a site to build on is also an option that should be approached with care. It must be located within an area which the government have approved for commercial development; you may need to verify what can be built before you commit to a purchase. Additionally, sites which have not been previously built on may need to be connected to the main sewerage system and have electricity supplied. If these facilities do not already exist on site it can be a costly business to add them. Your chosen site should also be considered in relation to what you are going to build and who is likely to live in or use it.

- **Council Permission**

The local government will have strict rules on the building of new properties or even the major modification of existing ones. Before you purchase any site or property it is essential to make sure you are familiar with the local rules and practices. It is the local government who will decide whether the project you envision can be carried out or not; every effort should be made to comply with their requests and keep them happy. This will make your build go much smoother.

- **Finance**

The many different finance options have already been discussed. However, as this is a property development, some of the suggested finance options may not be possible; for example a traditional mortgage is not an option. It is also worth noting that banks are a little more cautious when it comes to lending for property development. The loan to value percentage on a property development rarely goes higher than 70%; this is 70% of the land cost and 70% of the build cost. In real terms this means that you will need more of your own cash to get the project off the ground than you would if purchasing a real estate investment.

It is for this reason that many property developers find themselves agreeing to hard money or other, short term funding. This can cause an issue if the property takes longer than expected to complete or you are struggling to sell the property.

Of course, before you can arrange suitable finance you will need to work out a budget. For this you should list all items of expenditure, including the purchase of the land and associated costs. It is also advisable to make an allowance for unforeseen issues. Other than the finance you receive you will be reliant on your own funds; a property development cannot usually supply an income until it has been completed. This is why it is important to budget for every eventuality; you do not want to run out of funds prior to completing the project!

- **Architects**

The fees associated with an architect creating your design and submitting, revising and re-submitting these blueprints to the planning office can run into thousands. Unfortunately, this is a necessary part of the process, architects are supported by surveyors who will assess the land and confirm the structural integrity of key parts of the build. Not only will these professionals ensure your building is structurally safe, they will liaise with your builders to ensure the plans are adhered to and the planning regulations are enforced. This is essential as you are very likely to have a visit from the building inspector to sign off the build before it can be officially used.

Architects and other professional costs should be allowed for when working out your budget. Alongside designing the building for you they should be able to advise on current energy regulations and the best way of making your property energy efficient; or you may prefer to explore the options regarding a self sustaining building.

- **Builders**

It will be essential to have a team of qualified and trusted builders on your project. It is not possible or desirable for you to spend all your time at the site; even the architect who will supervise the build will not be able to watch the builders all the time. If you have a firm that you already use and trust it is advisable to use their services again; providing they are giving you a fair price. Otherwise, it will be necessary to ask friends and the developer contacts you have been making as to who they use; personal recommendation is the best way of choosing any business professional.

- **Tax Implications**

There are a variety of tax savings available to most new builds and development projects; there are also some taxes which only apply to this type of project. It is essential to utilise the services of a tax professional to ensure you maximize your tax position and minimize the tax due; the more funds you can save the more there will be available for your project.

Property development has the potential to provide a high return on investment but it is essential to purchase the site in the right location, the right economic climate, work out a budget and stick to it and, most importantly; use all available resources to ensure you complete the project. Development projects are one of the first casualties in a period of recession; you do need to keep an eye on the economic climate.

Chapter 6 – The Art of Flipping Houses

Flipping houses is not a new phenomenon; people have being buying, renovating and selling properties for years. Many homeowners are technically flipping their house after living in it for ten or twenty years; the improvements they have made over that time period have helped to increase the value of the home.

Flipping house is, generally a shorter term objective. Houses are purchased because they need renovation, or the buyer can see the opportunity to enlarge the house in a sympathetic way. Sometimes it is simply possible to redecorate a house and increase its value on the back of rising property prices. Once the renovations, redecorations or extensions are completed the house will be returned to the market at a significantly higher price than was paid for it. The difference between the buying and selling price should cover the cost of improving the property and all legal and other fees associated with the buying and selling of the property; with a little planning there should be a profit left which can be ploughed into the next property.

The following tips will ensure you successfully flip any house:

- **Finding a Property**

Some of the best properties on the market are the ones which have been foreclosed on; these properties are usually available at auction and can sell for much less than the retail value. This may be because the property is not in the best of condition, however; it is often because the bank is only interested in recovering enough funds to cover the outstanding mortgage. When purchasing at an auction it may not be possible or feasible to visit the property before you buy it; therefore, buy with caution!

It can also be beneficial to establish good relations with some of the local real estate agents; they will be able to advise when a potential property is coming onto the market and you may be able to purchase it before anyone else has the opportunity to view it. If you utilise this service, be sure to look after your real estate agent!

Whatever property you choose to purchase you must be certain that it is well below market value for the area it is in. If you do not do this then you are likely to make a loss when you sell the property.

- **Funding**

In order to purchase a property to flip you need to have some funds available. The best scenario would be to have enough cash available to simply purchase the property; but this is unlikely as you are seeking to build a real estate investment portfolio. The finance options discussed in chapter 1 still apply to a property being purchased with the intention to flip it. However, you do need to be aware that banks are less willing to lend on a property that needs to be flipped – this is because the asset is not necessarily as secure as a standard property and you may be stretching yourself to afford it. If it all goes wrong and you are unable to sell the house you have flipped you may be looking at having to pay two mortgages.

- **Location**

As with any property investment, the location is crucial. You should only ever buy a property in a desirable location; this will ensure you are able to sell it at the end of the process. Some of the best bargains can be had in the up and coming neighbourhoods.

It is also beneficial, if possible, to buy a property in a location near you. This will mean much less travelling daily as you administer the necessary repairs.

- **Condition**

To flip a house you need to locate a property which wants redecorating, a little renovation; or possibly the addition of an extension. You do not want a property development project where the house will need, to all intents and purposes, tearing down and rebuilding. If you are not an expert then make sure you take someone with you who is; you need to check structural integrity, electrics and the plumbing.

- **Repairs**

The point of purchasing a house to flip is that there is work which can be done to improve its value. The question you must ask yourself, when entering a potential property, is which repairs can you do yourself and which ones can you afford to pay a professional to do? More importantly, is there anything that needs doing which does not fall into one of these categories?

Most experts will agree that, in any situation, the work will end up costing more than you think it will. When estimating repair costs it is advisable to add 15% to your estimate; this will be closer to the real cost.

When calculating repairs it is essential to estimate the cost of upgrading or remodelling the kitchen and possibly the bathroom. These are the two rooms that will sell any property.

Finally, when it comes to selling the property make sure it is returned to the market at a fair price. If you have completed your sums correctly, this price will provide you with a profit. Marketing it at a fair price will ensure it sells quickly; once you have finished renovating it you do not want to hold onto it for any longer than you have to! You are then free to move onto your next project.

Chapter 7 – Managing & Diversifying your Portfolio

The aim of developing a real estate portfolio is to ensure you have sufficient properties to provide a good passive income. There are several key attributes that your portfolio must have to ensure it provides the income you want and deserve:

Property Management

Every property you own needs to be managed; all properties need to be insured and certain appliances must be safety checked at least annually. You will also need to be available if there is an emergency to organise a plumber, electrician or some other emergency response. On top of this it is essential to keep your property let and well maintained; this means visiting the property at least twice a year to check your tenant is happy and that the property is being looked after. Of course, if a tenant vacates the property then you will need to advertise, check and decide on a replacement; this will involve a fair amount of paperwork as tenancy agreements have to be drawn up and deposits held securely. In some cases you also have tenant s which stop paying the rent and need to be persuaded to leave your property.

Whilst this may seem manageable for one or two properties it will be incredibly time consuming the more properties you own and lease. This demand on your time will also prevent you from expanding your portfolio and achieving your goals.

It is, therefore, common practice to assign your houses to a property management team. This may be a specialist firm which will deal with all the day to day running of your properties, or, it could be a team of people recruited by yourself and working directly for you. If your portfolio is small it is usually better to utilize the services of a professional firm, once your portfolio is significantly big enough and can support the additional cost of wages payments you can consider having your own team who will report directly to you.

Whichever path you choose, it is essential to enlist the help of others. This will ensure you are able to continue to build your empire and to enjoy the passive income being created.

Portfolio Management

Your portfolio is your collection of properties and managing this may be different to managing the actual properties. If you have investment properties in several categories, such as residential and industrial you may find that one property management team are unable to look after all your properties. This is usually because of the different rules and regulations which need to be adhered to. This is less likely to be an issue if you have an in-house team.

In order to ensure your portfolio is being managed correctly you may choose to enlist the help of a portfolio manager. There role would be to monitor all your properties and report back to you regarding the current status of them, any issues or potential issues and to make suggestions on how to improve the use or yield of your portfolio. This role would need to be an employed position; they would work directly for you and their loyalty would be to you; this and a good re-numeration package will ensure they are dedicated to your business. This can be a particularly effective solution if your portfolio includes property development as well as residential or industrial leasing. Your portfolio manager will handle all the day to day activities and leave you to focus on strategy.

Diversification

In order to generate a passive income or build a real estate empire you need capital. Flipping houses is one of the quickest ways of building capital, providing you do it correctly. However, this is a higher risk and, not necessarily, a long term strategy. It is often a necessary first step to building your own capital reserves and avoiding or limiting your reliance on banks and finance houses.

Some of the properties you buy to flip may be too good and should be kept for residential leasing; others should be bought with this specifically in mind. The best real estate investors will have some property in each of the main investment types; the reason for this is threefold:

- **Limiting Risk**

Property development and flipping houses are far riskier investments than simply buying a property to let. However, they are also the opportunities that are most likely to provide significant returns on your investment. These riskier investments can also be beneficial when the economy is doing well; fewer people may be looking to rent as a good economy encourages people to buy their own property. These properties can be supplied via the development and flipping side of your portfolio. Equally, when the economy slows down there is much less demand for new or renovated properties, instead many people look to rent and your residential properties should do well. Finally, as the market starts to improve governments will encourage businesses to expand and new businesses to come in; these will be beneficial to the struggling economy. This is when your industrial and residential properties can do extremely well.

Having a range of properties across all the investment types should make it far easier for you to stay afloat during economic downturns and flourish in the upturns.

- **Increasing Returns**

Owning property in each of the investment types will not just help you to survive a recession; it will ensure you have the right property available when required to make a significant profit. The strong base that a range of property can provide you with; means, that you should always either have funds available or be able to access them should another opportunity arise. This may not even be within the real estate market.

- **Tax Implications**

Owning properties across the entire range of investment types will provide you with the ability to minimize your tax payment. Different types of property attract different taxes and it is usually beneficial to be able to offset one tax against another; of course, you will need to speak to a tax specialist to get the best advice and maximize your returns.

When considering the diversification of your portfolio it is important to consider moving away from a local base. Once you have established a good foundation and have a little security you will find it just as easy to invest in a property on the other side of the country as in your own back yard. Spreading your portfolio across different states will help to insulate you against market variables; even in a recession some parts of the property market remained buoyant. Of course, as with all property investment it is essential to research the market and know what you are purchasing; prior to committing to anything.

No matter how successful you have become or what you are purchasing you should continue to follow the principles described in this book. The value of any property can decrease and a badly conceived purchase can have a serious, detrimental effect on your real estate portfolio. Always complete your research and draw up a budget before committing to any project.

Creating a real estate portfolio will take time and plenty of hard work, there will be set backs along the way but you should learn from each one. When you have successfully built a real estate empire you will be able to consider trying your hand at a different kind of business; this will be made possible because of the income and security generated by your real estate investments. New ventures can be approached in the same way as any real estate purchase and can, over time, generate a substantial income of their own!

Chapter 8 – Common Mistakes to Avoid when Investing in Real Estate

Investing in real estate can seem like an easy way to make money; this book should have shown you that this is not the case. There is money to be made but it takes hard work, dedication and patience to be successful. When first looking to invest in the property market it is very common to make the following mistakes:

1. Planning

The importance of planning cannot be overemphasized. Before any purchase is made you must know what your goals are and how you intend to achieve them. One of the biggest mistakes any real estate investor can make is to attempt to make up the solution as they go along; this approach is designated to fail as they will not have the information available to make informed decisions. Instead of working out a budget, the right property type and the location it can be tempting to purchase a property because the price looks good. Of course, this is likely to mean you will overspend and struggle to break even, never mind create a profit.

Planning is essential, you then pick the property based on the parameters you have set; the actual property is almost irrelevant! Treat property investment as what it is; a business.

2. Believing the Hype

There are an abundance of shows regarding flipping property or property development. These shows make it look very easy to transform a property and sell for a decent profit; they do not show all the hard work that goes in behind the scenes. The same is true for much of the literature that you find scattered around the internet. In effect these programs make real estate investment look like a get rich quick scheme. It is not!

To be successful you must be patient, organised and willing to take risks; even a calculated risk in property investment can result in huge losses and even destroy all the hard work you have put in.

3. **Going it Alone**

It can be very tempting to choose a property, renovate it and then either find tenants or put it on the market. However, you will be missing a huge amount of possibilities and placing your profit in jeopardy. To successfully buy and sell a property you need an attorney, a real estate agent and, almost certainly, a financial backer. If you are intending to build a business in real estate you will be doing this many times. The insight and assistance that these professionals can give you will make a huge difference to the success or failure of your business.

On top of this you will need builders, plumbers and electricians to complete the renovations and annual maintenance. Building a relationship with these tradesmen will ensure you have support on hand when you need it. Having the work completed by professionals will also avoid any issues with substandard work when you come to sell or lease the property.

4. **Research**

Investment properties often come up at short notice and an investor will need to act quickly to ensure they secure the property. Unfortunately this will provide little or no time to research the property, its location and the repairs it may need. This can be a recipe for disaster as the property could drain all your available resources; even then you may struggle to sell it.

In order to ensure you are always prepared for a deal that may happen; you should constantly research the property market. This will entail monitoring current market movements, up and coming neighbourhoods and average prices for the neighbourhoods within your desired vicinity. You should also make sure you are aware of any changes in regulations which may affect the way you purchase property or the types of property you purchase.

5. **Stick to Your Word**

Investment real estate is a surprisingly small circle; many people involved in this market know each other and your reputation will be built on word of mouth. There is no reason for you to fall out with another property investor as there are ample opportunities. However, should you confirm your intention to purchase a property and then be unable to follow through; it will be noted by others within the industry.

If you should repeat this procedure you will quickly earn a reputation for being unreliable and you will probably find you are missing out on the best opportunities. It is a far better approach to be honest and stick to your word; if you tell someone you are going to do something then you should do it.

6. **Volume**

When you first start in real estate investment it is easier to purchase a property and deal with it completely before moving onto the next. However, this is not going to turn your portfolio into a viable business. To succeed at property investment you need to keep several deals in the pipeline at all times; this does not mean you have to complete on all of them at the same time. What it does mean is that you will not miss out on a once in a lifetime opportunity and any deals which are not as good as they first appear will be seen for what they are and terminated.

7. **Multiple Options**

The property market can be extremely volatile, even seasoned professionals who have done all the necessary research can find themselves with a property that was perfect for flipping and is now too expensive for the market. For this reason it is essential to have multiple options. When you are planning your budget for the property be sure to consider what you would do if you could not sell it. Renting may be an option or selling on owner finance.

The important part of this is to be prepared and have multiple options at your disposal; then, no matter how a situation may change you know you have a way out.

8. **Estimating Renovation costs**

It is common practice for anyone to under-estimate the cost of fixing something. Whilst one item by itself may not blow your budget, several items can. The result can either be overspending on the property and not being able to make a profit or having to cut corners on other parts of the property and selling or renting something which is not up to the right standard. Either option will place a huge strain on your finances and can cause a knock on effect into any other investment properties you are currently dealing with.

The best way to avoid this becoming an issue is to estimate the cost of repairing something and then add at least 20% on top; this should cover the actual cost.

9. Finance

Most investors need finance in order to purchase the property and either start or build their real estate portfolio. However, they are a huge range of operations available regarding finance. If you have not completed your homework and verified the different types, particularly which one suits your needs best, it is likely that you will agree to the wrong deal.

Finance often comes with fees and penalties for early settlement; interest rates can also vary wildly depending upon the lender and your own credit record. In fact some lenders have a very small presence in the real estate investment market and will struggle to provide you with a decent deal.

Remember, every penny you save in your finance package is an extra penny profit.

10. Marketing

A successful property investor does not just buy real estate and either rent them or renovate them. They also sell them and can build them. But, whichever type of investment you pursue, you will need customers. One of the biggest mistakes you can make is to not market your business; you may assume that the management company or the real estate agent will handle all of this. They certainly will for each sale or rental, but they are not interested in advertising your company as a whole and building your reputation; they have their own reputation to see too.

Letting potential buyers, sellers and even renters know about you and your business will give you more credibility and increase your profile. This will ensure that anyone you deal with will know you are a serious business which looks after its customers and provides a quality service. Without proper marketing you will always struggle to generate the right level of interest in one of your properties.

11. **Overpaying**

It is much easier than you think to pay too much for a property. There are several reasons why this may be the case:

- Your heart rules your head; falling in love with a property or being able to imagine yourself growing old in a specific place is not a good enough reason to purchase a property. You must look at every purchase rationally and from a business perspective.

- You rush into a purchase as you have got your finances ready and worry that someone else will get the property you have seen. If this is genuinely the case then you may have found a good property at a right place. Equally, you may be competing to purchase a property with someone who wants it as a home and is prepared to pay whatever to get it.

- You allow yourself to believe the hype; this may be that a property is in an up and coming area or that it is a very desirable area. Whatever the hype, you will only believe it if you have not done your research correctly.

There are many other reasons why you might pay too much for a property; as a beginner to the real estate market it will not hurt to watch a few deals progress to assess whether you would have been right to go for a property or not. This will help you to learn to trust your judgment.

12. **Over-Committing**

The more properties you have the more potential income you have. Your ultimate aim might be to have ten properties or a five million portfolio. This is an acceptable aim, but not one which should be rushed. It is quite possible, by accessing every available bit of finance through a variety of channels that you will simply overstretch yourself; you will grow too big to soon.

Whilst this might not become an issue, it will only take one house to be vacant for an extended period of time for you to encounter financial difficulties and risk losing it all. Every property you purchase must be assessed to ensure it will produce an adequate income and cover its costs; as described in chapter 3.

Over-committing was one of the biggest factors in so many real estate investors losing everything during the last economic recession.

13. **Bad Finance**

You will, by now, have realised that there are lots of different ways in which you can finance your next property purchase. However, think carefully before signing up to any deal; in your eagerness to secure the funds you may engage in bad finance. This does not mean there is anything wrong with the funds you receive; it simply means that the terms of the finance are not as attractive as those you could have chosen.

Of course, there are other reasons why you may have chosen a specific finance deal and these reasons might outweigh the additional cost of a deal. Again, adequate research will ensure you get a good deal and do not waste part of your profit in interest charges and other, ancillary costs.

14. Taxes

As a real estate investor you are running a business and you will need to record your income and expenditure, plus any other, relevant charges. These figures can then be used to calculate the tax due on your earnings. It is important to keep accurate records and to be aware of the tax implications of each of your properties; this way you will not be sent a tax demand which you can simply not afford.

Every state has its own rules regarding taxes and real estate investors; it is important to check your local rules and regulations to ensure you conform. It is also advisable to be aware of the capital gains tax and how much it could cost you if you decide to sell one of your properties.

Many people find it beneficial to use the services of an accountant or financial advisor.

15. Self Managing

Just like trying to do everything yourself, managing your property or properties yourself will leave you likely to fail as a real estate investor. This is because you do not have the time to look after the demands of all your tenants and build your own business whilst staying abreast of the latest market developments.

A property manager will check potential tenants and deal with the day to day issues of your tenants without needing to disturb you; leaving you free to focus on the bigger picture and what you need to do next.

16. Deferring Maintenance

It will be incredibly tempting to save costs by not replacing a worn out boiler until it has broken completely or until you have the funds available. However, this type of approach will cost you more in the long run. Tenants whose needs are not met will vote with their feet and simply leave at the end of the agreement.

It is also likely that if you do not pay out and repair something while you can then you are likely to both have something else go wrong and end up needing to replace an item rather than repairing it; this will increase the drain on your finances.

Staying on top of the maintenance will help to keep your tenants happy and prolong the amount of time they are likely to stay in your property.

17. Being Ruled by Your Heart

You have already seen the risk of overpaying if you let your heart rule your head. However, there are other complications which can arise if you adopt this approach. Approaching a property with your heart will make it more likely for you to see the property as a home. You may then attempt to redecorate and redesign the property according to the furniture and decor you can imagine being part of your dream home.

All of these things can add a significant cost to your property purchase and can even make the difference between making a profit or not. It is essential to remember that you are buying a property to rent; choose the property carefully and keep your expenditure to a minimum.

18. Dithering

People will often tell you stories regarding how badly a real estate investment went for someone they know; this can be due to lack of planning; in particular people have a tendency to simply dive in. Many investors purchase the property first and then decide what to do with it; this is never a good approach and will leave you open to prohibitive costs.

Although it is diving in which normally gets a mention, dithering can be just as costly. Delaying making a decision can cost you the property you were after. This is only likely to be an issue if you have not completed your research and are unable to decide whether a property is a good investment or not. Staying on top of market changes is an important part of being a real estate investor; it will ensure you are always ready to react to the right deal.

19. **Buying the Wrong Property**

Sometimes this is an inevitable outcome and a part of the learning curve. If you have bought a property which is wrong for your portfolio or has limited potential for income and tenants then the best thing you can do is off load the property as quickly as possible. It is preferable to do this for a profit but if not, at least for the same price which you paid for it. This will minimize any financial impact.

A lack of research or following your heart instead of your head are the most obvious reasons for buying the wrong property, but sometimes, it can actually tick all the right boxes and still be wrong. This is an experience that most real estate investors have at some point and simply need to learn from and move on.

20. **Education**

Because anyone can buy and sell a house it is often believed that it is not necessary to have an education or be educated to be a successful real estate investor. However, as already said, this must be treated like the business it is. If you have studied business at school or college then you will be able to apply this working knowledge to the real estate industry; it will help you know how to run a business.

Educating yourself in business management will allow you to develop strategies which others have not thought of, it will ensure you look at your real estate investments as the business they are and provide you with a good knowledge of general business concepts.

If you did not do well at school then there are plenty of adult course which can be completed, an education will prevent you from making many, costly, mistakes.

21. Expectations

Real estate investment is not a get rich quick scheme and it is not an easy option. You need to be constantly on the ball regarding market developments and potential properties. There will be pressures and demands from your properties and your tenants, in fact, there is probably always be something which needs your attention.

None of these challenges are insurmountable, but you must be prepared for them and prepared to work hard to make the most of your resources

22. Give Up on a Bad deal

At times you will purchase a bad deal, this can happen even if you conduct all the research and reviews possible. The important thing regarding a property which is not good for your portfolio is to have the courage to admit it was a bad purchase and get it back on the market. This can sometimes be difficult as you may wish to continue to prove others wrong, or even because you are trying something different and are convinced it will work out.

Whatever the reason, it is essential to remember that your real estate investment is a business and to assess each property regularly, not just at the time you purchase them. The global and local economy can affect your property and what was originally good investment may no longer be. If your property is not performing as it should then it should be fixed, if possible, or sold.

23. Advice

There are hundreds of people who will advise you on the right approach to real estate investment. Unfortunately, although many of them have good intentions, unless they have experience of the real estate industry it may be better not to heed their advice. There are others, who will appear to be well versed in the industry but who are actually making their money by scamming anyone new to the industry. It is best to seek advice from close family or friends who understand business and by attending the real estate seminars hosted by genuine professionals.

Whoever you turn to for advice, starting out in the real estate investment world will be a steep learning curve and you should be ready for that!

24. Rent Increases

In the euphoria of getting tenants into your property or properties it can be easy to focus on the next project and leave your management team to look after the existing properties. In general this is a good idea, but, it is essential to know what you expect from your management team and to check in regularly that they are living up to your expectations. This is your income they are looking after and if they cannot do it to the standard you require there are other firms who will.

It is best to complete a checklist to discuss with them, at least monthly. This will ensure you stay abreast of any developments and you can make sure they are following your guidelines and instructions.

One important detail that is very easy to overlook is the rent. It is much better to add small increases each time the lease is renewed, or at set intervals, than it is to suddenly need to dramatically increase the rent as you realise it has not been done for years and your income is static while your overheads slowly climb!

25. **The Cash reserve**

One of the biggest mistakes newcomers to the real estate industry make is to not have a cash reserve. This is essential to allow you to meet you financial obligations if your property is vacant, or if you have to make repairs in an emergency. A cash reserve also gives you the upper hand; you do not need to give in to the demands of a tenant just to ensure they stay in your property; you can afford to take your time picking the right tenant and, if you decide to sell, you can hold out until you get the right offer.

Conclusion

Real Estate investment should be approached in the same way you would approach any business, every decision should be made after studying the options and making an informed choice. Following the basic guidelines in this book will allow you to invest in a variety of properties successfully, ultimately it is possible to create a passive income which will allow you to have as much free time as you desire. This free time can be used to enjoy life with your family and friends or to invest in other projects and passions; something that would not be possible without the security or a regular, passive income.

Unless you have a large amount of financial backing then it is advisable to start by flipping properties and building your own cash reserve; this can be used to fund income earning property. Ideally you should aim to build your portfolio as quickly as possible, but, this should be balanced with a sensible and realistic approach. Do not overstretch yourself and always keep a little in reserve to cover emergencies or unexpected expenditure. This book is not the definitive guide; the system that works well for one person may not achieve the same results for someone else. The guiding principles, information and common mistakes should be read thoroughly and understood; it is these principles which should be used to guide you when making your own decisions. Provided you follow due diligence and do your research then the path you choose will be the right one.

Of course, any investment can go down in value as well as up; assuming you have done your research and are prepared then, the best thing you can do if things start to go wrong is not to panic and remember that the real estate market will always bounce back. Property investment is generally a long term commitment.

Investing in real estate is becoming an increasingly popular pass time; this is partly due to the ability to see your purchase and control it. Stocks and shares are generally more liquid but it is difficult to visualize them or control them fully; in contrast every part of your property can be controlled and adjusted by you at almost any time. This makes it feel like a safer option and makes it an appealing way to generate an income whilst increasing your net worth.

Possibly one of the greatest aspects of real estate investment is that it is possible for anyone to invest and potentially make money. Even those with very little, who do not wish to wait while they save the necessary funds, can invest in group schemes and obtain smaller rewards; hopefully this smaller rewards will lead to bigger things in the future.

You are now ready to enter the world of property investment and you should be determined to make the most of it. Follow the guidelines and make sure you keep accurate notes of all income and expenditure; this will make completing your tax return easier; you do not wish to fall foul of the tax office! In addition, ensure you always spread your risk by having different types of investment property; this will help to protect you from the ups and downs of the economic market.

Finally, no matter what you are faced with, be sure to stay positive, every set back is an opportunity to regroup and change your tactics, to learn and improve your methods for the future. Patience, perseverance and time will be the most important criteria for you to master if you are to achieve a passive income from real estate investment.

Made in the USA
Middletown, DE
13 November 2016